MY DREAM TO BE A

Luna loved to dream of dancing, imagining herself as a graceful ballerina. But one morning, while flipping through the newspaper, she found something that could make her dream come true.

THE ANNOUNCEMENT

Luna sat at the kitchen table, flipping through the newspaper, when her eyes landed on something amazing. An announcement for a national ballet competition caught her attention. A famous ballerina was coming to town! This ballerina was known for her breathtaking leap, a move that made her look like she could fly. Luna's heart raced as she imagined herself performing that same leap, soaring through the air with grace.

That night, Luna couldn't stop thinking about the competition. She tossed and turned in her bed, picturing herself in a sparkling tutu, dancing on a grand stage in front of an excited crowd. Her imagination ran wild as she dreamed of twirling and leaping, just like the ballerina she read about. The idea of becoming a ballerina filled her with hope and excitement.

The next morning, Luna woke up filled with determination. She ran to her dresser and grabbed her piggy bank, shaking it eagerly. The coins rattled inside, and with a swift motion, she smashed it open. She counted every coin, and it was just enough to buy her first pair of ballet shoes. Luna couldn't wait to get started on her journey to becoming a ballerina.

THE FIRST STEPS

Luna slipped on her new ballet shoes and stood in front of the mirror. Her heart pounded with excitement, but her legs felt shaky as she tried her first twirl. It wasn't perfect-she stumbled and nearly fell-but she caught herself just in time. Luna took a deep breath and tried again, her eyes focused on the dream ahead.

Every day after school, Luna practiced her ballet steps. She would twirl, leap, and stretch for hours. But it wasn't always easy. Sometimes her legs ached, and she felt like crying when she stumbled or couldn't get a move right. But no matter how hard it got, Luna refused to give up. She would always stand back up, brush off the tears, and try again.

Luna's hard work began to pay off. Slowly but surely, her leaps became higher, her twirls smoother, and her movements more graceful. She felt herself getting stronger, and with every day that passed, she got one step closer to her dream. The national ballet competition was fast approaching, and Luna knew she had to be ready.

OVERCOMING CHALLENGES

As the competition day drew near, Luna felt nervous. She knew she had worked hard, but doubts still crept into her mind. What if she wasn't good enough? What if she forgot her steps on stage? These thoughts filled her head, but Luna shook them away. She had come too far to let fear stop her now.

In the final week before the competition, Luna practiced harder than ever. Her body ached, and her feet were sore, but she kept pushing forward. She even practiced the famous ballerina's leap, trying to perfect it before the big day. It wasn't easy—she fell more times than she could count—but each time, she got up and tried again.

The night before the competition, Luna lay in bed, thinking about everything she had gone through. Her heart pounded as she imagined stepping onto that stage, with all eyes on her. She took a deep breath and reminded herself of all her hard work. No matter what happened tomorrow, she had already achieved so much by never giving up.

THE BIG STAGE

The day of the competition finally arrived. Luna stood backstage, her hands shaking with excitement and nerves. She peeked out from behind the curtain and saw the big stage in front of a full audience. Taking a deep breath, she reminded herself why she was there. Her dream wasn't just about winning it was about doing something she loved.

When Luna's turn came, she stepped onto the stage, her heart racing. The lights were bright, and the crowd was silent. She took her starting position, remembering every practice session, every fall, and every leap. Then, the music began, and Luna moved gracefully, twirling and leaping with all her heart. This was her moment, and she was ready.

As the performance reached its peak, Luna prepared for the final move-the leap she had dreamed about. She took a deep breath, bent her knees, and pushed off the ground with all her strength. Time seemed to slow down as she soared through the air, her heart soaring with her. In that moment, Luna wasn't just dreaming of being a ballerina-she was one.

QUIZ

Circle the correct answer

What inspired Luna to want to become a ballerina?

A) Watching a ballet movie

B) Reading an announcement in the newspaper

C) Seeing her friend perform ballet

What did Luna do after deciding she wanted to become a ballerina?

A) She joined a ballet school

B) She smashed her piggy bank to buy ballet shoes

C) She asked her parents for ballet lessons

How did Luna feel when she started practicing ballet?

A) Confident and perfect

B) Nervous but determined

C) Frustrated and wanted to give up

What was the hardest move for Luna to master?

A) A graceful twirl

B) The famous ballerina's leap

C) Standing on her toes

Made in United States
North Haven, CT
20 February 2025